Gee's Bend

by Elyzabeth Gregory Wilder

FOUNDED 1830

NEW YORK HOLLYWOOD LONDON TORONTO

SAMUELFRENCH.COM

IMPORTANT BILLING AND CREDIT REQUIREMENTS

All producers of *GEE'S BEND* *must* give credit to the Author of the Play in all programs distributed in connection with performances of the Play, and in all instances in which the title of the Play appears for the purposes of advertising, publicizing or otherwise exploiting the Play and/or a production. The name of the Author *must* appear on a separate line on which no other name appears, immediately following the title and *must* appear in size of type not less than fifty percent of the size of the title type.

Gee's Bend received its world premiere on January 21, 2007 as part of the Southern Writers' Project at the Alabama Shakespeare Festival
Geoffrey Sherman, Producing Artistic Director

PRODUCTION NOTES

"God has blessed us here in Gee's Bend." Those were the first words spoken when I sat down in the living room of Mary Lee Bendolph on December 26, 2004 to talk with the four quiltmakers who had graciously allowed me to interview them. Just as the character Sadie talks of leaving her door open to others, the women of Gee's Bend have left their door open to me. They have allowed me access to their stories, answered countless questions, and taught me about the strength of the human spirit.

This is not a play about the quilts. Rather, the quilts become the backdrop for a much bigger journey. The characters are meant to be a composite of the women I have talked to and read about. Many of the women in Gee's Bend marched across the Edmund Pettis Bridge on Bloody Sunday, they drank from forbidden fountains, quilted out of necessity, had children when they were much too young, and lived in marriages with men who were angry and overwhelmed by the world. However, the spirit of Mary Lee Bendolph has found a home in the character of Sadie. For that, I am grateful.

When working on the music I encourage you to avoid a polished "gospel" sound. For these women, singing is an extension of prayer. The sound is very raw and organic and comes from a deeply private place. The songs that are included in the script are all songs that are sung in the community and they were selected because they inform the scenes. If additional music is needed for transitions, may I recommend 'Take Me to the River", "Wade in the Water", "Give Me My Flowers", and "Look Where He Brought Me From." All of the music should be sung a capella and should underscore the scenes and transitions..

The play works best when it is done simply. One costume for each time period is sufficient. Because the play moves quickly blackouts should be avoided if possible. Sadie's journey is told through the key that she is given by Macon. The final moment of the play is perhaps the most important in that journey. The action of digging up the key is Sadie's acknowledgement that times are changing. When she puts the key in her pocket we never know if she is going to use it. What we do know is that she is prepared. This simple moment is imperative to the completion of her journey.

This is the first play I've written that was not born of my own imagination. With writing a story based on fact comes responsibility. As I left that night in 2004, Mary Lee said to me, "Just write it honest." It is my hope that I have done just that.

Elyzabeth Gregory Wilder
October 2008

The world premiere of ***GEE'S BEND*** was produced by the Alabama Shakespeare Festivl; Geoffrey Sherman, Producting Artistic Director. It was presented on January 21, 2007 with the folowing cast:

SADIE . . . . Roslyn Ruff

NELLA . . . . Margo Moorer

ALICE, ASIA . . . . Maura Gale

MACON . . . . Billy Eugene Jones

Directed by Janet Cleveland

Musical direction by Brett Rominger, scenery design by Michael Schweikardt, costumes by Rosa M. Lazaro, lighting by Kathy A. Perkins, sound by Brett Rominger and casting by Elissa Myers Casting, Paul Fouquet CSA. The stage manager was Sara Lee Howell.

PART I

Scene 1

(1939. In darkness, a song is heard. The singing under-scores the monologue.)

WOMEN. *(singing)*

How we got over.

How we got over, oh my Lord.

You know my soul looks back and wonder

How we got over.

(The sun is setting on the banks of the Alabama River. The sounds of nature can be heard in the background. **SADIE PETTWAY***, 15, stands face toward the fading sun.)*

SADIE. God has blessed us here in Gee's Bend.

I had a dream. A vision that's come to me more than three nights now. It was just like the story pass down from my great granddaddy. He tell about the walk they made. Winter of 1845. Came all the way down from North Carolina. A hundred of them on foot. Mr. Pettway, the man who own us, he say my granddaddy too young to make the trip. Want to leave him behind. But his mama wrapped him in a quilt and sewed him into the bed ticking and hid him up in the wagon.

Only in my dream, it was me sewed up inside. Sewed up so you can't see, can't breathe. They picked me up, still wrapped like the baby Moses and placed me in the river. And the river carried me away. Floating like.

WOMEN. *(singing)*

How we got over

How we got over oh my Lord

When my soul look back and wonder
How we got over.

SADIE. Been scared of that river all my life. It's a mighty river. A dark river that can eat you up, you don't respect it. You respect it and it keep you safe. Protect you from what's on the other side.

'cept today it was different. Different, cause I wasn't scared. I just let myself float. Have faith that you will protect me. I pray about it. Ask you to bring me the meaning.

WOMEN. *(singing)*
I been through trials
I been through trials and tribulations
Makes my soul look back and wonder
How we got over.

(**SADIE** *takes a deep breath. She is covered in water. This is her Baptism.*)

End scene

Scene 2

(**ALICE PETTWAY** *[34] is piecing a new quilt. Her daughter,* **NELLA** *[17] pulls balls of cotton from a field sack, stretches them out, then places them on a big piece of quilt backing that lays on the floor.*

SADIE *stands, reading from a piece of newspaper that lines the wall. The newspaper pieces create block patterns on the walls.)*

SADIE. *(reading)* "*I got more confidence in my land than I had in my own wife," one of them told me. And that is saying a lot, for the Pettways of Gee's Bend are a very moral people.*"

ALICE. Would you stop that?

SADIE. It's my favorite part.

NELLA. We heard it all before.

SADIE. How many people you think read about us?

ALICE. All of New York City, I guess.

NELLA. Why a newspaper man from New York want to be talking about us?

SADIE. Cause we lovely people, like it say.

ALICE. You getting good at your reading.

SADIE. I been practicing.

NELLA. Drive me crazy with all that.

ALICE. You should be practicing too.

NELLA. Not me. I don't like to read.

SADIE. You don't like doing nothing. You read better if you go to school more.

ALICE. Now you know I need Nella here to help with the little ones.

NELLA. See? Mama needs me.

SADIE. When we gonna move into our new house?

ALICE. Your daddy say they have it finished before they start the planting.

NELLA. Then maybe we won't have to be listening to Sadie reading off the walls all the time.

SADIE. Mama likes my reading.

NELLA. Read the same thing over and over. Probably ain't even reading it. Probably got it in your head by now.

ALICE. We gonna have walls that shine.

SADIE. I put newspaper up and read anyway.

ALICE. Girl, you better not be putting newspaper up on my clean new walls.

NELLA. We gonna have real walls, Sadie. Don't need newspaper to keep the wind out when you got real walls. Maybe then we have some peace around here.

SADIE. You gonna be missing my reading.

ALICE. Sit yourself down. I want to finish piecing this before the boys come in.

NELLA. I sent the little ones down to pick us some jewberries for supper. Told 'em not to come back til they had two buckets full.

ALICE. It ain't the time for jewberries.

NELLA. They don't know that. Keep 'em from being underfoot while we working.

SADIE. *(laughing)* They be too scared of Nella to come home without them jewberries.

NELLA. Them little ones making me crazy. Mama, you need to train them better.

ALICE. Tried training you. Didn't do no good. You start having your own. You see.

(**SADIE** *pick through a pile of old work clothes.*)

SADIE. Mama, there ain't nothing here to cut.

ALICE. You find a place.

SADIE. Done been wore out. Got patches on the patches.

ALICE. Cut around them.

SADIE. Them boys tear up they clothes.

ALICE. Reverend say he gonna ask you to read at church on Sunday.

SADIE. See Nella? All that reading's good for something.

NELLA. You go on and read. I keep to my singing. I'm good at singing.

ALICE. Can't read at church 'less you been Baptized anyway.

NELLA. Can't help I don't have visions like you do.

ALICE. Can't be Baptized till the Lord calls you.

NELLA. I been trying. I go out there in the woods. I listen. But all I hear is nothing. Be a fool standing out there waiting for the Lord to speak to me.

ALICE. You stay out there long enough, he'll bring you his word.

NELLA. Bet them people over in Camden laugh when they see us out there wading in the river, talking to Jesus.

ALICE. They laugh all they want. The Lord put that river between us for a reason.

NELLA. Bet they was laughing at you, Sadie. When they seen you being baptized.

SADIE. Don't bother me none.

ALICE. Ain't no good waiting for you over there.

NELLA. They got some nice looking mens over there.

ALICE. Like I say.

NELLA. There ain't nobody good over here.

ALICE. None of them mens is gonna be wanting to be marrying you, you don't learn how to cook. How to sew.

NELLA. I ain't good at none of that.

ALICE. Can't be good at nothing you ain't never tried.

SADIE. Nella good at killing pigs.

NELLA. Don't you be talking 'bout them pigs.

SADIE. Mens hear 'bout you butchering them pigs they get scared off.

NELLA. Mama the one make me take after them pigs. Ain't my fault they had got killed.

ALICE. Nobody saying you got to be butchering. Saying you need to learn how to tend house.

NELLA. I get too hot cooking over that fire. Boiling them clothes to clean.

ALICE. You afraid to sweat.

NELLA. Mens don't like a woman all sweaty like that.

ALICE. Don't like a woman can't cook they food and wash they clothes neither.

NELLA. Macon see me doing the wash yesterday.

SADIE. He laugh when he see Nella hanging her drawers up on the line.

NELLA. Did not.

SADIE. Laughing cause your drawers so big.

NELLA. I tell him it was your drawers I was hanging out to dry. He smile at me.

SADIE. Why you think that man be looking at you?

NELLA. Cause I seen him. He sure ain't looking at you, with your old knotty head.

SADIE. My head ain't knotty. Look at you.

NELLA. I look good.

ALICE. Hush, with the both of you.

SADIE. I thought you say there ain't no mens worth nothing over here.

NELLA. I don't want that man.

SADIE. Do so. I think Nella hang her drawers out on the line on purpose.

NELLA. Where else they s'posed to dry?

SADIE. But he don't give her the time of day.

ALICE. That boy too old for you. He a man. He come sniffing around here I take after him with my broom.

SADIE. He ain't doing nothing.

ALICE. Not yet he's not.

SADIE. He just being nice.

ALICE. That's what I'm afraid of. You stay away from that boy now. Hear me?

End Scene

Scene 3

(**SADIE** *sits on a quilt with* **MACON PETTWAY** *[25].*
They are having a picnic. He is charming.)

MACON. That was some good pie you made.

SADIE. Mama gonna be mad she find out I used up all the sugar.

MACON. Make me all fat and happy.

SADIE. Glad you like it.

MACON. Sound real good reading at church today.

SADIE. I don't like standing up in front of all them people.

MACON. Nella sure don't have no trouble singing in front of folks.

SADIE. She always showing off. Not me. I don't like folks looking at me.

MACON. I sure like looking at you.

SADIE. My mama's gonna whip me raw she find out I gone off with you.

MACON. Your mama sure do get on to you 'bout things.

SADIE. Just how she is.

MACON. You ain't tell her about us?

SADIE. No. She say I need to stay away from you.

MACON. I take you back then.

(**MACON** *starts to get up, but* **SADIE** *stops him.*)

SADIE. She won't be missing me til supper.

MACON. You give her some of that pie and she won't be mad. *(pause)* Looking good there, Sadie.

SADIE. Boy, what you looking at me for?

MACON. I can't tell you you look good?

SADIE. Don't be looking at me. I done told you I don't like it.

MACON. Then I guess I have to go looking at Nella.

SADIE. Don't be looking at her neither. I seen you waiting round out by our house.

MACON. You never even look my way.

SADIE. Ain't true.

MACON. Glad you look my way today.

SADIE. *(changing the subject)* Where you say you get this truck?

MACON. From the co-op.

SADIE. Ooo, you gonna get in trouble they find out you take off with they truck.

MACON. I didn't take off with it. I borrowed it. Co-op doing so good we might go buy us another one.

SADIE. You is doing good.

MACON. They let me drive it over to Camden this week.

SADIE. All that way?

MACON. Didn't take the road. Took the ferry. Drove that truck right up on it. We there fast.

SADIE. I be too scared to get on that ferry boat in that truck. That ain't right, a little old flat bottom skiff carrying a big old truck.

MACON. We just float across. Take our things in to sell in town. The co-op been good for us here. Means we got some say on who we sell to. How much we sell for. I already done made back what the man be furnishing to me.

SADIE. Already?

MACON. Yeah. What you gotta do see, is you got to put a couple of bales back. You go in and you say, I got my eight bales for you. So when he say you short one bale, you say, "No sir, see I got me two more bales out in the truck." That way you come out ahead. Don't matter how much you bring in, they always say you short. That's why you gotta be smart.

SADIE. Bet that make that man mad.

MACON. Look like he swallow a gnat. But I come out of there with some money in my pocket.

SADIE. How much he give you?

MACON. Ain't saying.

SADIE. You ain't got no money.

(**MACON** *flashes a few dollar bills.* **SADIE** *grabs for them, laughing. He crams them back in his pocket, just out of her reach.*)

SADIE. That ain't fair.

MACON. Gonna be more where that came from, I get my land working. You mark my words, Sadie. This is just the beginning for Gee's Bend. Them days of working other people's land. Having people take our things.

SADIE. Nella still has nightmares about when old lady Rentz come riding through.

MACON. Wanted to bring you out here. Wanted you to see this.

SADIE. Ain't nothing but cotton. You think I ain't never seen cotton before?

MACON. That's my cotton. A hundred acres in all. Got some upland for corn and some lowland for cotton.

SADIE. My daddy got some of that government land, too. Our new house look so nice.

MACON. Talked to the man from the Farm Administration. He signed me up. Pretty soon, I'm gonna be driving a truck all my own. What do you think about that?

SADIE. I think you talking big.

MACON. It's true. You just see.

(**MACON** *hops up.*)

SADIE. Where you going?

MACON. See this here? I gonna have a house right here.

(**MACON** *starts mapping out his house.*)

MACON. Right here's the living room. And the kitchen, with a real cook stove. Won't be cooking over a fire no more. Right here is a room for the babies.

SADIE. Babies?

MACON. Oh, yeah.

SADIE. How many babies you be wanting?

MACON. Least a dozen.

SADIE. Twelve head of children?

MACON. My mama had eighteen to live.

SADIE. I don't know about that.

MACON. That's why over here there be a nice room for me and my wife. Nice and big.

SADIE. All that?

MACON. All mine. Yours too.

SADIE. Mine?

MACON. I'm gonna marry you.

SADIE. You can't marry me. You a Pettway.

MACON. Most everybody around here a Pettway. Or they mama a Pettway. Or they marry a Pettway. But that ain't what we started with.

SADIE. Still.

MACON. You holding out for something not a Pettway, you gonna be dying alone, girl.

(**MACON** *pulls out a key.*)

MACON. See this here. This here gonna be the key to our new house. I'm gonna build you a house, Sadie. You gonna live in it with me. And I'm gonna protect you.

SADIE. You think so?

MACON. I know so. What man ever give you a house before?

SADIE. Ain't no house yet.

MACON. Will be.

SADIE. How I know you ain't lying?

MACON. You hold onto that key. That key is my promise to you. I'm gonna give you a house and make you my wife. You'll see. I think you might better get on back to your mama.

SADIE. I could stay a little longer.

(*They kiss.*)

End Scene

Scene 4

(**SADIE** *is trying out the key.* **ALICE** *is scrubbing the floor.*
NELLA *is snapping peas. They are in their new house.*)

NELLA. Why you gotta be scrubbing the floors? They already clean. Ain't even lived here long enough to make 'em dirty.

(**ALICE** *notices* **SADIE**.)

ALICE. What you doing over there?

SADIE. Nothing.

ALICE. Where'd you get that key?

SADIE. Found it. Just wanted to see if it worked.

ALICE. Why you need a key?

SADIE. Never had a lock before.

ALICE. You sit yourself down here.

SADIE. Why?

ALICE. Cause I say.

SADIE. Ain't you gonna lock our door?

ALICE. What do we need a lock for?

SADIE. Somebody might come up in here and take our things.

NELLA. Like when old lady Rentz come up in here collecting on her credit. Wouldn't have gotten nothing there been locks on the doors.

ALICE. A lock on the door wasn't going to stop that woman from getting what she wanted.

SADIE. Course somebody come up in here trying to take our things, we just put Nella and her butcher knife after 'em.

NELLA. Somebody come up in my house I got a mind too.

ALICE. They want something I got, they just ask. Ain't putting no lock on my door. You leave your door open for people, they leave theirs open for you. Now put that key away and sit yourself down.

SADIE. Yes, ma'am.

(ALICE pulls out a bag of scraps and hands it to SADIE.)

ALICE. Want you to take some of them scraps and start piecing you up something.

SADIE. You never let me piece before.

ALICE. You getting to that age.

SADIE. I want to make me some pretty quilts.

ALICE. You piece it like you see in your mind, they be pretty. My mama put me to quilting 'bout your age. You do good. You always had a good head for things.

SADIE. Why you don't let Nella start piecing?

NELLA. Cause I ain't got no babies.

SADIE. I ain't got no babies.

ALICE. You will. You big.

NELLA. You getting fat.

SADIE. I ain't fat.

ALICE. You been laying up with Macon.

SADIE. We ain't done nothing.

ALICE. That man put a baby inside you. I see it in your face.

NELLA. Got all round.

ALICE. Folks seen you riding around in that truck.

SADIE. Nella!

NELLA. Being doing more than just riding.

SADIE. We just talk after school sometime.

ALICE. Can't go back to school now. No, not the way you is.

SADIE. I like school.

ALICE. All you need to know now, you learn here. Time you learn to quilt. You having a baby.

End Scene

Scene 5

*(**SADIE** and **MACON** stand outside their new house. Sadie's stomach is now round and full. She holds a quilt over her arm and a flour sack filled with her belongings.)*

MACON. Well. Go on inside. It ain't gonna eat you up.

SADIE. I'm just looking at it.

MACON. Nice, right?

SADIE. You built it good.

MACON. For me and you and our babies.

SADIE. Never been away from home before.

MACON. This your home now.

SADIE. Been sleeping next to Nella my whole life.

MACON. You sleep next to me. I keep you nice and warm.

SADIE. Nella, she do have cold feet. Like to put 'em on me at night just to make me mad.

MACON. You won't be having no cold feet. I wrap you up good.

SADIE. Made us a quilt. For our bed. A wedding quilt.

*(**SADIE** holds out the quilt.)*

SADIE. It ain't much.

MACON. You sewed it good.

SADIE. Took just about everything in mama's scrap bag to make it. But I washed 'em all up. Pressed 'em out. Pieced it together. But I look at this house and it look too nice to be putting my ugly quilt inside. My daddy say not in his whole life he ever think he be owning a house this nice.

MACON. I get this land so I got something to show for all the work I do. I get this land, so my wife and my children always got a home.

When we was little, we out in the fields, working somebody else's land. I be just a little thing when I see old Van de Graff's son come riding through here on his horse. Naked as the Lord made him. That man was crazy. He go up and down the rows of cotton tossing pennies into the dirt. Yelling to the mens, "Here chickie, chickie, chickie." And them mens come crowding around, pushing at one another hoping they find a penny or two that man done thrown down.

I see my daddy down on his knees and I say to myself, "Won't never see me like that." Van de Graff sees me just standing there and yells out, "Pick up them pennies, boy." But I don't move. Everybody stops. Looks. "Pick 'em up." He starts throwing them pennies, one at a time. Hitting me in the head. But I stand there, stone still. 'til that man come round on that horse and kicks me to the ground.

We get home that night and my daddy just about beat me dead. Tells me I made a fool a him. Like I ain't been taught better. He beat me cause he want me to learn.

But I make my own promise that day. I promise myself I won't take no hand out from no body. You be the one on the ground, the only place you got to look is up. So that's what I do. I say to myself, You keep looking up, one day you be there. And here I am. With a new house and a new wife and a new baby coming up.

Now come on, now. Less you plan on sleeping out here in the yard.

(**SADIE** *hands him the key.*)

MACON. I give that to you.

SADIE. And I'm giving it back.

MACON. We done married. You can't be giving it back.

SADIE. I marry you. But I ain't got no use for locks on my doors. My mama say we blessed to have so much. Tell me you leave your door open for other people, they leave theirs open for you. You share your blessings. I come live in your house. I have your babies and cook your suppers. But my house will be an open house.

(**MACON** *takes the key.*)

SADIE. Promise me.

MACON. It's just a key.

SADIE. Promise me there won't be no locks on my doors.

MACON. I promise.

End Scene

PART II

Scene 1

(1965. Sadie's house. The sound of rain can be heard outside. **ALICE** *[61] is working on a quilt. Her daughter,* **NELLA** *[44], is ripping apart old clothing for quilting scraps. They sing as they work.)*

WOMEN. *(singing)*
Somebody's knocking at yo' door.
Somebody's knocking at yo' door.
Oh-oh sinner, why don't you answer?
Somebody's knocking at yo' door.
Knock like Jesus.
Somebody's knocking at yo' door.
Knock like Jesus.
Somebody's knocking at yo' door.
Oh-oh sinner, why don't you answer?
Somebody's knocking at yo' door.

*(***ALICE*** stops, rubs her eyes.)*

ALICE. Listen to that rain. You remember to take the clothes off the line?

*(***NELLA*** pauses. Clearly she didn't.)*

ALICE. Nella!

NELLA. They was wet when I put them out. What does it matter if they get wet now?

ALICE. It'll matter when you don't have no clean clothes to wear.

NELLA. Oh they'll be clean. Good and clean.

ALICE. Girl, how you get grown without learning to quilt?

NELLA. Lucky, I guess.

ALICE. You had children, you'da learned to quilt.

NELLA. Lucky there too. I need a quilt, I go buy me one at the store.

ALICE. Who you think you is, buying you a quilt?

(**SADIE** *[41] enters. She is wearing a nice, but simple handmade dress which she is trying to button up the back.*)

NELLA. I gonna marry me a rich man. He buy me whatever I want.

ALICE. Ain't no rich men around here.

NELLA. I go to Birmingham. Where the men have good jobs. Get me one of them mens.

SADIE. You been saying that since we was children. You still here. And ain't no rich men as far as I can see.

(**ALICE** *hands* **NELLA** *a needle and thread, which* **NELLA***, without question, threads and gives back to* **ALICE.***)*

NELLA. You don't know who I be seeing.

SADIE. Them mens don't want you. They want some young thing they can spend they money on.

NELLA. They can spend they money on me just as good as anybody else.

ALICE. Turn down every man that asks.

NELLA. Can't help I'm particular.

ALICE. Better take what you can get.

NELLA. I'm not marrying some ol' farmer. Ain't gonna spend the rest of my life picking that cotton and working that hoe.

ALICE. You too good for that.

NELLA. That's right. All the smart men done moved away from here. Got theyselves good jobs. They keep leaving, pretty soon won't be no men left down here. Just our old tired selves picking peas and singing.

SADIE. Macon still here.

NELLA. He was smart, he'd be leaving too.

SADIE. You know Macon ain't gonna leave his land.

ALICE. Girl, sit down. You moving too much.

NELLA. I smell sweet potato pie. Ooo, I love sweet potato pie.

SADIE. You best keep your hands offa my pie.

ALICE. What you make a pie for?

SADIE. For Macon. His favorite.

NELLA. Sadie trying to soften him up.

ALICE. Gonna take more than a pie for him to let you go.

(**SADIE** *turns around to* **ALICE**.)

SADIE. Mama, can you get that button?

ALICE. What you put buttons up the back for?

SADIE. Looks nice.

(**ALICE** *buttons the dress.*)

NELLA. I never seen that dress before.

SADIE. Been saving it for something special.

NELLA. Why you don't make me a dress like that?

SADIE. I thought you only buy from the store.

ALICE. See, now, if you had learnt to sew you be making your own.

SADIE. You sure you won't come too?

ALICE. You not getting me out in that weather.

NELLA. Gonna ruin that dress.

SADIE. I pull something over me. I want to look nice.

ALICE. Wanna finish piecing before we go on back to the house.

SADIE. Ooo, that's real nice.

ALICE. 'bout done. Be done faster if Nella help.

NELLA. I'm helping. I thread that needle for you. Can't quilt without no needle and thread.

SADIE. I work on it with you.

(**SADIE** *pulls out a new quilt.*)

See what I done.

(*She holds up the quilt, with bold green patches.*)

NELLA. That's too bright.

ALICE. I like it.

SADIE. Stayed up finishing it last night. Gonna put it on the bed. Been so cold this winter had to put all the good quilts on with the children. You think Macon'll like it?

NELLA. Now you know don't matter what a quilt looks like. It's what you do up under it that counts.

(*NELLA laughs.*)

ALICE. That's right, Sadie. Keep the man happy. These quilts could tell some stories.

NELLA. I know that's right.

(*They all laugh.*)

NELLA. Is that what you been praying about, Sadie? I hear you down in the woods moaning this morning.

SADIE. You dirty minded.

NELLA. That's what I heard.

SADIE. I go there to pray and here you go making it into something dirty.

ALICE. Nella, you stop with that.

SADIE. What you doing snooping round my special place, anyway? You so nosy.

NELLA. Everybody in town can hear when you take to moaning.

SADIE. Needs some time to myself.

ALICE. She talking to the Lord. You could use a little more time with him yourself.

NELLA. Thought some animal was dying from the sound of it.

SADIE. Can't sleep. Dreams be coming to me.

NELLA. There she go.

SADIE. Keep waking up at night thinking I'm drowning.

ALICE. You don't turn your back on what the Lord bring you in your sleep. Means something. I tell you what.

SADIE. I ask the Lord to bring me the meaning.

(*MACON [51] enters. He is wet.*)

SADIE. Lord, look at you.

MACON. Coming down hard out there.

(**SADIE** *takes his wet coat.*)

SADIE. Now you know you ain't s'posed to be getting chilled. You hear what the doctor say.

MACON. That doctor gonna tend to my field, while I sit up?

ALICE. Get him dried up before he goes tracking through the house.

(**SADIE** *helps him out of his shirt, while* **ALICE** *pulls out an old quilt.*)

MACON. Thought the ferry was gonna break loose down river, it's moving so fast.

SADIE. Don't like you being on the ferry, the weather bad out.

MACON. Had to get home to my wife's sweet potato pie.

SADIE. It was supposed to be a surprise.

NELLA. She trying to soften you up.

SADIE. Nella! Pull this over you. Keep the chill out.

(**ALICE** *hands the quilt to* **SADIE** *who then wraps it around* **MACON**. **SADIE** *tenderly rubs his chest with salve.*)

MACON. I can smell your sweet potato pie clear cross the river. It smell that good.

SADIE. They ain't fix the truck?

MACON. Can't do nothing for it. Had to talk to the man at the bank.

SADIE. Oh, Macon...

MACON. They give me a loan until the cotton come in this summer.

SADIE. But we had plans for that money.

MACON. You know I don't like owing.

SADIE. Guess you gotta have a truck.

MACON. Can't hardly keep up as it is. I hate walking in there, my hat in my hand.

(**MACON** *coughs.*)

SADIE. You gonna catch your death. Put this on.

(**SADIE** *gives him a plain, but new shirt.*)

MACON. Where's my old workshirt?

(*Just as* **NELLA** *rips apart a tattered workshirt.*)

MACON. Who said you could tear up my shirt?

NELLA. Don't look at me.

SADIE. It's wore out.

MACON. Can't put nothing down without you tearing it up for a quilt.

SADIE. I just made you a new shirt.

MACON. Don't want a new shirt. I want that one.

SADIE. You'll look nice for tonight.

MACON. Sadie, I'm wore out.

ALICE. Listen to you. The man sick and you want him going out in this mess?

MACON. You don't need to be going either.

SADIE. But he come all this way. Everybody gonna be there.

MACON. I got a bad feeling about all this. That man likes to stir things up.

SADIE. I put on my new dress.

MACON. I do like that dress.

(**SADIE** *models.*)

SADIE. With buttons up the back.

MACON. Where you getting money to be making new dresses and new shirts?

SADIE. Sold one of my quilts to the lady over at the General Store. Said her niece was getting married. Give me two dollars worth of fabric. It's nice, see?

ALICE. Let her go. I stay here and do your supper.

SADIE. Please, Macon. Nella'll go with me.

NELLA. It's cold out there.

MACON. She got some sense.

SADIE. He gonna tell us about registering to vote.

MACON. Just gonna stir things up. Nobody gonna let you vote.

SADIE. People been doing it.

MACON. Have to prove to them you can read.

SADIE. How you think I heard about him coming? Cause I read it in the paper.

NELLA. She always reading something.

SADIE. I read anything they give me. I can read just as good as anybody else. Made it all the way to the eighth grade. *(playfully)* Would have finished too if I hadn't have met you. Started having your babies. Eight head of children I had for you. Good, strong children.

(MACON playfully smacks her on the butt.)

MACON. Watch yourself now.

SADIE. I'm tired of just reading about things. I want to be there. See it with my own eyes.

MACON. Might get more than you bargained for. What about all them people turning up dead? People getting beat in the streets? You read about that?

SADIE. He's a peaceful man.

MACON. Don't mean the others are.

SADIE. The children been fed. They all sleeping. Please Macon.

(The two face off for a moment. MACON can't resist her and finally gives in.)

MACON. Don't know why I bother saying no. You just gonna do as you please.

SADIE. Thank you.

MACON. Now, you ain't going down there alone.

SADIE. Nella?

NELLA. What you looking at me for?

SADIE. Say you'll go.

NELLA. It's gonna cost you.

(SADIE grabs her coat.)

SADIE. Nella say she'll go.

ALICE. I'll put your dinner out.

MACON. You mind yourself.

SADIE. I'll come straight back.

> (**SADIE** *hands a coat to* **NELLA**. *She takes one of her quilts in her arms.*)

NELLA. You always in a hurry.

SADIE. The church'll be full up we don't hurry.

MACON. I don't want to hear nothing 'bout you being tired tomorrow.

SADIE. Thank you.

> (*Excited,* **SADIE** *gives him a kiss.*)

NELLA. What about the pie?

SADIE. I'll bake you your own pie.

NELLA. Oh, it's gonna cost you more than just a pie.

> (*They exit.*)

End Scene

Scene 2

(At church. **SADIE** *and* **NELLA** *squeeze into a church pew. They sit in silence for a moment.)*

NELLA. It's cold up in here.

SADIE. Here.

*(***SADIE*** *spreads a quilt out over their laps.* **NELLA** *pulls it up around her.)*

SADIE. Don't be taking it all.

NELLA. He come all the way to Gee's Bend to visit, you think they could have warmed the place up. Put some more wood on the stove.

SADIE. That man get to talking this church'll be on fire. Won't even be thinking about the cold.

NELLA. We don't freeze first.

(Pause.)

NELLA. I can't see.

SADIE. What you need to be seeing for? We here to listen.

NELLA. Well, I want to see. I come all the way down here in the rain to see Dr. King, then I want to *see* Dr. King.

SADIE. Never seen this many people in church before.

NELLA. That's cause people want something. People think they gonna get something, they show up.

SADIE. That ain't true.

NELLA. Then why all these people here? Not cause they come to get them religion. Last time this many people come up in here was back when they was giving out the land. Then people show up.

*(***SADIE*** *gives* **NELLA** *a voter registration form.)*

SADIE. Take it.

NELLA. What?

SADIE. Your papers. For voting.

NELLA. You registering?

SADIE. Said I would. You too.

NELLA. I don't know about that.

SADIE. Take it. Gotta have it all filled out when you hand it in.

NELLA. They gonna make me read?

SADIE. You be ok.

NELLA. I don't like reading in front of people.

SADIE. You sing in church all the time.

NELLA. That's different.

SADIE. You can sing in front of the whole church, but you can't read a few words to some man?

NELLA. I'm good at singing.

SADIE. I be there.

NELLA. I don't know.

SADIE. Everybody taking the ferry over to Camden. Going down to the courthouse. Everybody going to be registering.

NELLA. They gonna be mad seeing all us walking up in there.

SADIE. What they gonna do? Not like we some poor old share cropper answering to somebody. We own our land. Can't put us out.

NELLA. They find a way. Mark my words.

SADIE. They ain't gonna do nothing.

NELLA. You say that.

SADIE. What they got to be mad about. We just going up and signing some papers.

NELLA. Girl, you just about stupid sometimes. You think you can just walk up in there, sign some papers and walk out? How old you now?

SADIE. You know how old I am.

NELLA. Forty-one years old and you don't know how the world work? Ain't nothing ever that easy.

SADIE. Then fine. Don't go.

(Pause.)

NELLA. He ain't coming.

SADIE. He'll be here.

NELLA. We been waiting more than two hours.

SADIE. Where you gotta be? Just hold on now. Weather's bad. You can't hardly get down them red clay roads when the weather's bad.

NELLA. He's one good looking man.

SADIE. He's married.

NELLA. Don't mean he ain't good looking.

SADIE. Don't talk that way.

NELLA. Don't look at me. You the one putting on your good dress.

SADIE. Nothing wrong with looking nice.

NELLA. Nice enough to wear your good dress. I need to find me a man like that.

SADIE. You just need to find a man. You old.

NELLA. I ain't run off with the first man that ask, like you.

SADIE. Macon's a good man. Macon work hard. He provide for us.

NELLA. Just so you cook his dinner, sew his clothes and lay up with him at night.

SADIE. He my husband.

NELLA. You can't tell me you don't think about other men.

SADIE. Ain't no other men to think about. They all just like him. Breaking they backs. Macon just trying to provide. He been good to me.

NELLA. Macon find out you planning on marching in Camden, he ain't gonna let you go.

SADIE. Take the ferry to Camden all the time.

NELLA. You know you scared of that water.

SADIE. The Lord take me across. The Lord knows it's important. He'll get me there safe.

NELLA. Macon won't hardly let you come tonight. What make you think he gonna let you follow Dr. King across the river?

SADIE. He don't have to know.

NELLA. You getting awful brave now, Sadie.

SADIE. You don't know Macon like I do. You gotta know how to handle him.

NELLA. I see how you handle him. Baking him pies, rubbing his feet.

SADIE. Nothing wrong with that.

NELLA. I'm just saying.

(*Pause.*)

SADIE. I'm taking that ferry.

NELLA. What you gonna do, Macon find out?

SADIE. How he gonna know?

(**SADIE** *looks to* **NELLA.**)

End Scene

Scene 3

(In Camden. In the background: sounds of a public place; the chatter of people, cars passing by, etc.

SADIE *and* **NELLA** *stand in a crowd of people. It's a brisk, but sunny day.)*

NELLA. I heard there's a man coming round to buy some quilts. He a minister.

SADIE. What do he want with our quilts?

NELLA. I don't know. He paying cash money though. You got lots a quilts you can sell.

SADIE. I don't know if I want to be selling off my quilts. I love my quilts.

NELLA. You make more. If I had a quilt, I be selling it off.

SADIE. Look at all the people, Nella. You ever seen so many people?

NELLA. Thought that ferry was gonna sink, they so many people on it.

SADIE. I told you.

NELLA. What?

SADIE. Told you everybody was going.

*(***NELLA*** inspects her voter registration card.)*

SADIE. Let me see it.

NELLA. No.

SADIE. Just let me see.

NELLA. It got my middle name.

SADIE. You think I don't know your middle name?

NELLA. Why they have to put that on there?

SADIE. Cause it's official.

NELLA. It's a ugly name.

SADIE. Nobody gonna be looking at it but me and the man when you vote.

NELLA. Should have told them I didn't have no middle name.

SADIE. Then you'da been lying.

(**NELLA** *looks at the card.*)

SADIE. You did real good with your reading.

NELLA. I just try to think about church. Pray the Lord help the words come out.

SADIE. Now you glad you came?

NELLA. Nice seeing my name typed out like that.

SADIE. Better put it up safe.

(**NELLA** *tucks it away in her pocket.*)

NELLA. Best be heading back to the ferry.

SADIE. You always wanting to go.

NELLA. Don't like all these people standing around.

SADIE. Hush, now. Look at Dr. King.

NELLA. What he doing now?

SADIE. He up there at the water fountain.

(**NELLA** *cranes her head to see.*)

NELLA. Too many people.

SADIE. Look here.

(*They peer through the crowd.*)

NELLA. That man just wants to die.

SADIE. He saying something.

NELLA. Can't he read what the sign say? Say "White's Only."

SADIE. That's why he doing it.

NELLA. I can't look.

SADIE. Then you oughta take yourself back home.

NELLA. I'm not leaving you.

SADIE. Then you stand here and be strong. Dr. King, he be strong for us, so we be strong for him.

(*They stand in silence for a moment, watching Dr. King drink from the fountain.*)

SADIE. That water look so good.

(**SADIE** *takes a step toward the water fountain.* **NELLA** *grabs her.*)

NELLA. Sadie…

SADIE. Let go.

NELLA. What you think you're doing?

SADIE. Going to get me a drink of water.

NELLA. You best stay put.

SADIE. I'm thirsty.

NELLA. The sheriff's just looking for a reason to let loose. You got children at home you got to be thinking about. You find yourself under the jail. Or worse.

SADIE. They can't jail us all.

NELLA. They die trying.

SADIE. I'm gonna get me a drink of that water.

NELLA. Just cause Dr. King drink from that fountain don't mean you can.

SADIE. Just cause Dr. King drink from that fountain means everybody can.

(*Through the crowd,* **MACON** *appears.*)

MACON. Sadie!

SADIE. Thought you was working.

MACON. Somebody say they seen my wife on the ferry this morning. I say no, my wife at home with the children.

SADIE. Mama home with the little ones.

MACON. Should be out plowing. But here I gotta come chasing after you. Get in the truck.

SADIE. I just come over to register. Me and Nella, we got our cards, see?

(**SADIE** *tries to show him her registration card, but he knocks it from her hand.*)

SADIE. Macon…

(**SADIE** *bends down to pick it up.* **MACON** *grabs her by her arm and stands her up forcefully.*)

NELLA. Macon, don't.

SADIE. What you gonna do?

MACON. Taking you home.

SADIE. Macon, you're hurting me.

(**MACON** *realizes what he's doing and releases her.*)

SADIE. We just came out to see Dr. King.

MACON. You seen enough. You think them white folks up in them stores ain't keeping track. You don't think they won't be showing up at our front door. Burning our houses. What you doing is dangerous.

SADIE. We just waiting for a drink of water.

MACON. We take care of this at home.

SADIE. I haven't got my drink of water yet.

NELLA. Just go with the man.

MACON. Now I let you go down to the church to hear the man speak. Don't do this now, Sadie. Please. Now, we going home.

SADIE. I'm thirsty.

MACON. You what?

SADIE. I'm going to get me drink of water.

MACON. You better step back.

(**MACON** *grabs her, but she pulls away.*

They stare at one another. A moment. Another.

SADIE *moves toward the fountain defiantly. She bends down and drinks. She stands up.*)

NELLA. What's it taste like?

SADIE. Like a little piece of heaven.

(**SADIE** *wipes her mouth and walks past* **MACON.**)

End Scene

Scene 4

(Her back to us. **SADIE** *stacks quilts. She is wearing her nice dress again.*

There is an eerie calm about Sadie. She works with purpose. **MACON** *coughs.)*

SADIE. You should've stayed in the bed.

MACON. Ain't time for that.

SADIE. That cough's getting worse.

MACON. I'm fine.

SADIE. You ain't been breathing right. Can't afford you being sick.

MACON. Can't afford no doctor neither.

SADIE. I get mama to make you up some more salve for that cough.

(He coughs again. She turns to reveal a cut across her forehead.)

MACON. Why you pulling out all them quilts?

SADIE. Gonna hang 'em out to air.

MACON. Oughta burn 'em up, them ugly things.

SADIE. They keep you warm. They still good. Got a preacher coming to buy 'em.

MACON. Nobody gonna be paying good money for them old quilts.

(She stacks the quilts in a pile.)

SADIE. Maybe not.

MACON. People talking 'bout what you did yesterday.

SADIE. Word spreads.

MACON. Saying you gone crazy.

SADIE. Ain't crazy.

MACON. Gonna have to put you up at the state hospital, you keep carrying on.

SADIE. They do it too, if they ain't be scared.

MACON. Make me look bad. People be saying I can't control my wife.

SADIE. I just wanted a drink of water.

MACON. Hope it was worth it.

SADIE. It was worth the beating you gave me.

MACON. Now you know I didn't wanna do it. But you earn that beating.

SADIE. I been your wife more than 25 years now. In 25 years you never raise a hand to me.

MACON. Never had to.

SADIE. Now you just like all them others. You a big man now.

MACON. Fix your hair. Folks don't need to see you looking like that.

SADIE. Don't want them seeing what you done?

MACON. I told you not to go.

(**SADIE** *looks at herself in the mirror. She take a bobby pin from her hair and pulls it back, leaving bangs to cover the cut on her forehead.*)

MACON. Don't know what's got into you.

SADIE. Just doing what I think's right.

MACON. You wearing your good dress to church?

SADIE. I'm not going to church.

MACON. It's Sunday.

SADIE. I know.

(**SADIE** *puts her coat on.*)

MACON. Where you think you're going?

SADIE. Going into Selma. Mama's going to cook your lunch.

MACON. What you think you're doing in Selma?

SADIE. The children all dressed.

MACON. Another march?

SADIE. I'll be home by supper.

MACON. There's nothing but trouble waiting for you there.

SADIE. What about when I come home? There be trouble here too? We just gonna march across the bridge. Ain't nobody gonna do nothing to make them mad.

MACON. You being there's enough.

SADIE. We got the right.

MACON. Since when did that matter?

(SADIE *slams a card down on the table.*)

SADIE. See that? That's worth all the trouble in the world, Macon. That card there, it means that I count for something. That what I think matters.

MACON. Well, just cause you got a vote out there, don't mean you got a vote in here.

SADIE. Tell me I can't go.

MACON. Don't do this, Sadie. Don't you see? It's for your own good.

SADIE. Tell me.

MACON. Go on.

(SADIE *looks at him.*)

MACON. Go!

(*She then takes the bobby pin out of her hair and pulls back her bangs, so that the cut can be seen across her forehead. She looks at him defiantly, then puts on her coat.*)

MACON. You walk out that door, don't you come back.

SADIE. The cornbread's warming in the stove.

(SADIE *gathers up her quilts and leaves.*)

End Scene

Scene 5

WOMEN. *(singing)*

> *Oh, Lord, I'm on my way*
> *My, Lord, I'm on my way.*
> *So blessed, I done died one time.*
> *So blessed, I done died one time.*

*(**SADIE** stands at the door, disheveled. Her eyes are swollen. She tries to open the door, but it's locked. Tries again. She knocks. Nothing.)*

SADIE. Macon? Macon, where you at? Open the door.

(she pounds on the door.)

My eyes. I can't hardly see. They put gas in our eyes. It burns real bad like. I need you to help me. It was real bad there. Bad like you never seen. They beat us, Macon. They was waiting and when we come up over that bridge they took after us. I put my eyes straight in front of me. Walk strong, I be thinking. Walk strong. I so busy looking ahead I don't see what come up from behind. Sky goes black and me, I'm on the ground. Taste the blood. But I know the hurt mean I'm still alive. They beat on us, then left us for dead. Folks in they stores all up along the way, they just stand there and watch. We cry out, but don't nobody do nothing to help.

Please, Macon. I know you say don't go. But I had to. That man, he be beating on me and I say, Sadie, you stand up. I ask the Lord to give me strength. That man might beat me down, but the Lord he raise me up.

I'm hurt, Macon. Please. Open the door.

(She wraps herself in one of the quilts and slowly sinks to the floor.)

WOMEN. *(singing)*

> *This old world, ain't none of my home.*
> *This old world, ain't none of my home.*
> *One of these days, I'm going home.*
> *One of these days, I'm going home.*

End scene

Scene 6

(NELLA, ALICE and SADIE stand at the road side. ALICE and SADIE hold their quilts in their arms. ALICE holds two quilts, nicely folded. Sadie's are in a bundle in her arms. Sadie is bruised and silent.)

NELLA. The sheriff say they didn't cut off the ferry because we was black. Say it's because we forgot we was black. Now how we supposed to forget we black? Look in the mirror every day. Somebody always there to remind us.

ALICE. So it was just gone?

NELLA. I get down there this morning and it ain't there. Everybody just standing there at the water looking. Like you look long enough, it gonna show up.

ALICE. I bet that sheriff over there on the other side just smiling.

NELLA. He say we don't like it, we can walk out of here the same way we come in. Got half a mind to.

ALICE. Where you gonna go?

NELLA. Get on a bus and head north. Maybe New York.

ALICE. Girl, the first time you feel that kinda cold you be back on the bus to Alabama.

NELLA. Won't get shot trying to register, that's for sure.

ALICE. There's more than one way across the river. Ain't that right, Sadie?

SADIE. Where's that man?

ALICE. Baby, you ok?

SADIE. He say he coming to buy our quilts.

NELLA. He a preacher. If he say he's coming, he'll come.

SADIE. Say he giving ten dollars a quilt?

NELLA. Cash money.

(SADIE drops the pile of quilts on the ground and begins folding them.)

ALICE. Say he give us ten dollars now and the rest when he sells them up in New York City.

SADIE. How much you think that be?

ALICE. Lord, I don't know. Ten dollars seem like a lot. But that preacher, he say they'll pay more. Gonna make us some good money.

NELLA. 'Bout time. Can't be depending on the farming no more.

ALICE. You can't sell off all your quilts.

SADIE. Why not?

(**SADIE** *folds her wedding quilt.*)

NELLA. That's your wedding quilt.

SADIE. It's ten dollars.

NELLA. You can't go selling that one. I remember you making it. You so proud of it. What'd Macon say?

SADIE. Don't matter what he say. These my quilts and I sell 'em if I want to.

ALICE. Hush with that talk.

SADIE. He a mean man.

ALICE. You make him mad? The doctor said he can't be getting upset.

SADIE. He put a lock on the door.

ALICE. A lock?

SADIE. I come home, all beat up and he lock the door. Leave me out in the cold like an animal. I pull my quilts off the line and make a bed on the porch. Been out there two nights now.

ALICE. Baby girl. You shoulda come got me.

SADIE. There ain't never been no lock on our door. We leave our doors open. Open to anyone who need to come in. And now he closed it up. He the one gonna be sorry.

ALICE. Don't say that.

SADIE. My babies see me out there last night. What they think, seeing they mama sleeping out like that?

ALICE. We go over there tonight and we talk to him.

SADIE. I won't say sorry.

ALICE. Don't be pig headed.

SADIE. I sleep out there every night, I have to. But that man won't hear me be saying sorry.

(**SADIE** *finishes folding the last quilt. She stacks them neatly.*)

SADIE. There it is. A hundred dollars. A hundred dollars take me a long way from that man.

End Scene

Scene 7

(Night. The room is dark. **SADIE** *climbs through the window. From the darkness.)*

MACON. Don't be breaking my windows.

*(**MACON** turns up the lamp to reveal him sitting there, waiting.)*

SADIE. Thought you'd be asleep.

MACON. Paid good money for them glass windows.

SADIE. Wouldn't have to come through the window if you ain't lock the door.

MACON. You wanna come in, all you got to do is ask.

SADIE. Ain't asking you for nothing.

MACON. Then you best be going on back outside.

SADIE. Soon as I say goodbye.

MACON. Goodbye?

SADIE. Saying goodbye to my children. They be scared they wake up and I'm not here.

MACON. Where you think you're going?

*(**SADIE** begins to pack her belongings in a pillowcase.)*

SADIE. Leaving, Macon. Wanted to tell the children I love 'em.

MACON. Won't get far without the ferry.

SADIE. I walk then. Get me a bus in Selma.

MACON. Gotta have money for the bus.

SADIE. Got me ninety dollars.

MACON. Where you get that kind of money?

SADIE. Sold my quilts. 'cept our wedding quilt. The preacher man didn't want that one.

MACON. Somebody give you money for them things?

SADIE. He say they nice.

MACON. Ninety dollars won't last you long.

SADIE. I get me a job.

MACON. Just like that.

SADIE. I do alright. Better than being here.

MACON. I provide for you.

SADIE. You lock me out of my own house.

MACON. How else you gonna learn.

SADIE. You promised. No locks on our doors.

MACON. It's for your own good.

SADIE. So is marching.

MACON. You got children to think about. A family. What makes you think the men that beat you on that bridge won't come here in the middle of the night and burn us out of our house?

SADIE. We own our land. They can't come up in here.

MACON. There are lines drawn. It's my job to make sure you don't cross them.

(**MACON** *begins to cough.*)

MACON. Get me some of that salve.

(**SADIE** *doesn't move.*)

MACON. Sadie.

(**MACON** *gasps for air.* **SADIE** *watches for a moment, torn between staying and leaving. She then drops her pillowcase and goes to help him.*)

End scene

Scene 8

(**SADIE** *hums as she tends to* **MACON**.)

SADIE. *(humming)*
If anybody asks you
Who I am
Who I am
Who I am
If anybody asks you
Who I am
Tell them I'm a child of God.

(**MACON** *lays in bed.* **SADIE** *sits at his side, dozing off.*)

MACON. Sadie.

SADIE. Can't hardly keep my eyes open.

MACON. Cover me up.

(**SADIE** *pulls a quilt over him. It's the wedding quilt.*)

SADIE. Oughta burn up this ratty old thing.

MACON. Glad you ain't sold 'em all.

SADIE. It's so tore up. I was proud of this ol' thing. Wasn't but fifteen when I made it.

MACON. For our wedding.

SADIE. You remember that?

MACON. You do good.

(**MACON** *coughs.* **SADIE** *opens a small jar filled with homemade salve.*)

SADIE. Wish I had learned more about mama's doctoring. She go out in the woods, pick her roots, cook 'em up. Make you all better.

MACON. You wearing that dress I like.

SADIE. Yeah.

MACON. You wear that when I go. You look real nice in that dress.

(**MACON** *lifts up his hand, shaking from the chills. Inside his hand is the key.*)

MACON. Take it.

SADIE. No.

MACON. It's yours now. All this.

SADIE. I can't.

MACON. I put that lock on to keep you safe. You don't know that, but that's what I did. Just lay with me, Sadie. Right here. I know you don't like the touch of me no more. Just for a minute.

(**SADIE** *hesitantly crawls in bed beside* **MACON**. *They lay together for a moment.*)

SADIE. You burning hot.

(**SADIE** *takes his old work shirt and wipes his brow.*)

MACON. I should have loved you better.

WOMEN. *(singing)*
If anybody asks you
Who I am
Who I am
Who I am
If anybody asks you
Tell them I'm a child of God.

(**MACON** *drifts off.* **SADIE** *takes the work shirt and begins ripping it into pieces.*)

Meet me, Jesus meet me.
I want you to meet me
In the middle of the air, oh yeah.
And if these wings
Should fail me
I want you to meet me
With another pair.

If anybody asks you
Who I am
Who I am
Who I am
If anybody asks you
Tell them I'm a child of God.

End Scene

Scene 9

(The Cyprus swamp. **SADIE** *stands in her special place. She is wrapped in the quilt made of Macon's clothes. She holds something in her hand.)*

SADIE. I come to ask you to forgive me Lord.

We buried Macon yesterday. I cried, Lord. People say they never seen me cry like that before. But I couldn't tell them that I wasn't crying because I was sad. I cry because I feel like you lifted a weight from me.

*(***SADIE** *opens her hand to reveal the key.)*

Macon give me this key when he ask me to be his wife. The key to our house. He was so proud, Lord. Say he gonna protect me. Promise that we live in an open house. The man that raise his hand at me, who put a lock on my door, that ain't the man I married.

Now I come and go as I please. I live in an open house. A loving house.

(She places the key in a mason jar.

She lays her quilt down on the ground and carefully kneels down. She digs a hole in the dirt, places the jar inside and covers it up.)

SADIE. They cut off that ferry, make it real hard on some folks. But it ain't been so bad. People leave us alone. Gee's Bend a peaceful place. We starting the Freedom Quilting Bee. Gonna be sewing for Bloomingdale's Department Store up in New York. Lord, you give us our quilts and the quilts give us our freedom. And we just have to try and ask you to help us, Lord. We be making our own money now. Don't need to be answering to the mens. For the first time. My life feel like it my own again, Lord. Like I live for me.

End Part II

PART III

Scene 1

(2002. Sadie [78], finds Nella [81], confused, standing at the river's edge.)

SADIE. I been looking all over.

NELLA. Now Sadie, you s'posed to be tending to the little ones. Mama said.

SADIE. We gotta get home, Nella. Asia gonna be waiting on us. We got packing to do.

NELLA. Where we going?

SADIE. Going on a trip. To see our quilts. They be hanging in a museum.

NELLA. What they be wanting with our quilts?

SADIE. That man from Atlanta come up in here. He tell us what we making is artwork. And he hang them up on the walls. Nice like, so everybody can see.

NELLA. Ain't never been to a museum before.

SADIE. Then you best get moving.

NELLA. Y'all go on without me. I gotta get to town.

SADIE. What you doing down by the river?

NELLA. The ferry ain't come yet. I been waiting for it, everyday. And it ain't come.

SADIE. Ain't no ferry.

NELLA. Usually be here by now. Willie must have fell asleep. Forgot to bring the ferry around.

SADIE. Willie dead.

NELLA. He died?

SADIE. That ferry ain't been here in 35 years.

NELLA. It was here yesterday. Me and Mama went in selling jewberries.

SADIE. Mama been dead.

NELLA. She died?

SADIE. Yeah. Everybody dead, but you and me.

NELLA. When's the ferry coming?

SADIE. It's not.

NELLA. But I gotta go see old lady Rentz. I got things to tell her.

SADIE. What you got to tell her?

NELLA. She stole our things, Sadie. I'm going over there to get them back.

SADIE. What she take?

NELLA. They didn't give us no warning. Nothing. Mr. Rentz, over in Camden, was the man doing the furnishing for us. But then Mr. Rentz dies and his widow decides she want it all back. I come running down the road. *Mama, they coming. They got wagons. They taking everything.* Mama standing there on the porch, big ol' butcher knife in her hand. She send the little ones in the house. She say, *Nella, take this knife. Want you to go out to the barn and kill them two hogs. The babies too. Take the knife and slit they throats. They ain't taking my pigs.* I love them baby pigs. *You big now. Go on.* All the way down the road, people standing on their porches and watching as the men ride through. Wasn't long before a man come with his wagon. Don't even speak. Just starts taking. Took mama's milk cow that was out in the yard, shovels and buckets.

He just about to leave when he hear them pigs back in the barn. They screaming something terrible. He looks to mama, standing there stone faced, and he smiles. He take off toward the barn. But then the screaming stops. And here I come, covered in them pigs' blood. He got one look at me and he take on off outa there.

'bout that time daddy come running in from the field. But it was too late. He chase after that man until he fell down in the dirt. The only time I ever seen my daddy cry. That man was broke down.

Mama roast them pigs, but I couldn't eat. Can't hardly stand the smell of pork. I do what mama say. But it ain't right.

*(**NELLA** stands looking out over the water. She is confused.)*

SADIE. Well maybe tomorrow it'll come. And you can tell the Rentz lady what's on your mind. We oughta go on home now.

NELLA. What if it comes and I'm not here?

SADIE. They'll wait.

(They pause for a moment, take in the world around them.)

NELLA. Nice, ain't it?

SADIE. Real nice.

NELLA. You hear them crickets?

SADIE. I hear 'em.

NELLA. They talking to us.

SADIE. What they saying?

*(**NELLA** shoots **SADIE** a look.)*

NELLA. I don't know. They crickets. How I know what crickets say? You crazy.

*(**SADIE** laughs.)*

NELLA. Can we wait a little longer?

SADIE. Just a little.

End Scene

Scene 2

*(***ASIA***, Sadie's daughter, 45, stands at the door. Nella is locked out on the other side. [Note:* **ASIA** *is played by the same actor who played* **ALICE***.] Several suitcases are in the middle of being packed up.*

Nella knocks.)

NELLA. Let me in. It's cold out here.

*(***ASIA*** *fumbles with the locks and opens the door revealing* **NELLA***.)*

NELLA. Must've done it wrong.

ASIA. I did it right.

NELLA. You do it right and it'd work. Been standing out there half the morning waiting for you to let me in.

*(***ASIA*** *takes the key from* **NELLA***, slips it in the lock.)*

ASIA. You the one doing it wrong. Try it again.

(But the lock doesn't work.)

NELLA. Told you.

ASIA. I'll do it.

NELLA. Go on. I'm wore out.

*(***NELLA*** *sits down on the couch.)*

NELLA. I let you back in.

*(***ASIA*** *locks the door, then closes it behind her. She fumbles with the lock. Tries again. After a moment, she knocks.*

NELLA *takes a piece of hard candy out of her pocket and carefully unwraps it, making no move toward the door.)*

ASIA *knocks again.)*

NELLA. Told you it don't work.

ASIA. Let me in.

NELLA. You believe me now?

*(***ASIA*** *pounds on the door.)*

ASIA. Aunt Nella. Open the door.

(**SADIE** *enters. She carries with her several items of clothing.*

ASIA *pounds on the door again.*)

SADIE. What's all that pounding?

NELLA. Asia locked outside.

SADIE. What on earth?

NELLA. Told her that key don't work.

ASIA. Mama, let me in.

(**SADIE** *opens the door.*)

SADIE. Here we are trying to get packed up and you off messing with that key. Now I best not be missing that bus on account of your fool self. Get in here.

ASIA. Must be the wrong key.

NELLA. I told you.

(**NELLA** *unwraps another piece of candy.*)

SADIE. Nella, you know you ain't supposed to be eating that. What the doctor say?

NELLA. My age, ain't the candy that'll kill you.

(**SADIE** *reaches into the pockets of Nella's dress and pulls out a handful of hard candies. She puts them in her own pocket.*)

NELLA. Don't you be eating my candy.

SADIE. You worse than the grandkids.

NELLA. Asia, when you gonna finish my hair? I can't be going out with half my head done. I gotta look good.

ASIA. You the one screaming every time I touch it.

NELLA. Can't help I'm tenderheaded. You be done by now you ain't messing with that old key you found.

(**ASIA** *begins working on Nella's hair.* **SADIE** *sorts through the clothes.*)

ASIA. Trying to find a key to fit that lock.

SADIE. The key to that door been long gone.

ASIA. You need a lock that works, Mama.

SADIE. What for?

ASIA. Cause you don't know who's roaming around outside is what for.

SADIE. I know every last soul down here. Anybody want to come up in my house, let them.

ASIA. Not with the ferry coming.

SADIE. That ferry ain't going nowhere.

ASIA. The ferry's coming and you don't know who all it'll bring. You need a lock on the door.

SADIE. My door hasn't been locked in 35 years. Last time I had a lock on my door was 35 years ago and a lock hasn't been on it since. Somebody want something of mine I'd rather them go through the door to get what they want then have my window's broke. I'd rather them go in my house and take my things than break my windows. They tear up my windows, I gotta hire a carpenter and he charge about fifty dollars an hour. Put a lock on the door and you come home and your window be tore up and your things be gone.

NELLA. This time they say it coming.

SADIE. They be saying that every year. And every year it don't come.

NELLA. I be the first one on it. Gonna take me a good ride across that river.

SADIE. Won't get me on that boat. I don't think that thing'll act right. It'll get bogged up. How they gonna get that big boat down through there? Water ain't that deep.

NELLA. Used to ride it.

SADIE. That when there was something worth seeing on the other side. Never did like it though.

ASIA. Now mama, you just being stubborn.

SADIE. What if that boat sinks? You know what live in that water? Snakes. I don't like snakes.

NELLA. You always been scared of them things. (*to* **ASIA**) Your mama used to wouldn't go to the outhouse after dark on account of the snakes.

SADIE. That's your fault.

NELLA. I tell her, snake come up out of that hole and lick you clean.

SADIE. You nasty.

NELLA. Last time she be in that river when she get Baptized. You so scared.

SADIE. I get in that water for the Lord and not nobody else. They left us alone all these years. Us on one side and them on the other. Fine by me. What these people be wanting with Gee's Bend?

NELLA. Somebody say they building a golf course.

ASIA. A golf course?

NELLA. That's what I hear.

SADIE. What we supposed to do with a golf course? Nobody I know play golf. Black folks got better things to do.

ASIA. A black man invented the golf tee.

NELLA. That's cause he tired of holding the ball while some white man try to hit it. That man got smart.

SADIE. Nobody want to go to Camden anyway.

ASIA. The children won't have to sit on the bus half the day. They just take the ferry across.

SADIE. You think they gonna drive a bus up on that ferry boat? Not with my grandbabies on board.

ASIA. They make it safe.

SADIE. I keep driving the long way, thank you. Be lots less trouble than what that ferry bring with it.

ASIA. Mama...

SADIE. I'm tired of talking about it. Don't touch that lock again, hear me? Now help me get packed up. If we ain't on the bus they gonna leave us behind.

(*ASIA starts folding the clothes and placing them in the suitcases.*)

ASIA. It was hard saying goodbye to my quilt.

SADIE. They take good care of it.

ASIA. I hope so.

SADIE. A quilt is meant to be shared.

ASIA. Makes me all excited thinking about seeing it up on that wall.

SADIE. You remember to get a camera like I ask?

ASIA. Already put it in your bag. I packed your good dress in case we have a nice dinner. And here's an extra sweater to take on the bus with you. Gets cold.

SADIE. Better put one in for Nella too. She always cold.

ASIA. Already did.

NELLA. I got a quilt they can hang up on the wall.

SADIE. Only quilt you got's a quilt I done made you.

NELLA. I still sell it to them.

SADIE. You can't go selling him my quilt.

NELLA. I wanna see my name up on that wall like yours.

SADIE. Well, then you should've learnt to quilt. You old pig head.

ASIA. My boss didn't want to let me off work. But I showed him that write up in the paper. About how our quilts were going to be hanging in a museum and he say it's alright.

SADIE. I sent a copy off to each one of the boys. They can't hardly believe we in the newspaper.

ASIA. My boss say when I come back he want to talk to me about being a manager.

SADIE. A manager. Ooo, Asia that's real good.

ASIA. It's a full time job. I tell I'm too old to be learning a new job, but they say they like the way I am with people.

SADIE. You always been good with people. You someone they can trust, cause you listen good.

ASIA. I've been thinking about moving us into Selma.

SADIE. Selma?

ASIA. I'll be making good money, Mama. And that drive's about to do me in.

SADIE. Been doing it for years.

ASIA. I'm getting too old.

SADIE. We all getting old, Asia.

ASIA. It's what I need to do.

SADIE. You grown.

*(There is an uncomfortable silence. **SADIE** busies herself with packing.)*

ASIA. I was thinking I might sell off my land.

SADIE. No, now, that dog won't hunt.

ASIA. You ain't heard what I have to say.

SADIE. I hear you just fine.

NELLA. Now you know your mama ain't gonna let you sell off that land.

ASIA. It's my land.

SADIE. You tell your brothers?

ASIA. No. What do they know about it? They aren't here anyway.

SADIE. They got responsibilities. They work hard.

ASIA. So do I. But it's just me here now. Just me here to take care of you and Aunt Nella and the kids. And I'm tired.

SADIE. Your daddy left it to you kids so you'd always have a home here. This house been real good to us.

ASIA. If I sell it, I still have a home. Buy us something nice. You sell this place. Move to Selma with us.

SADIE. What do I want with Selma?

ASIA. Be good to have Nella close to the doctor. Her mind's slipping.

SADIE. Doctor can't do nothing about that. Her mind's just wore out.

NELLA. My mind might be wore out, but my ears work just fine. Don't you be worrying about me Asia. I can tend to my own self.

ASIA. You can't take care of this place.

SADIE. I do alright.

ASIA. You don't need to be out in that heat, trying to keep up the yard. It's too much.

SADIE. I done it all my life. It's what makes you strong. Kids today get raised up without hard work. They ain't strong like we are. Can't do what we do. Don't know what we know. Nothing wrong with picking and plowing. We been picking since we been old enough to walk.

NELLA. Grandmamma take us out in the field with her. She a big woman. She say, walk behind me, I keep the sun off. And she did. She so big when she died they had to bury her in a piano box. Where they got that piano box from, I don't know. But that's what they did.

SADIE. Did not.

NELLA. You don't know.

SADIE. I stay right here, thank you.

ASIA. You could get good money with the ferry coming. People looking to buy it up.

SADIE. The ferry ain't coming.

ASIA. Junior sold off his piece.

SADIE. And what happen? Junior thinks he need a nice car, so he sell off his land. Junior wreck his car and spend off the rest. Now he ain't got no car and no land. You hold onto your land, you always got a place to go home to.

ASIA. Think about it, Mama.

SADIE. I done all the thinking I need to do. You ain't selling off your land. Me and your daddy worked too hard to get it.

ASIA. I'm not asking for your permission. I'm asking for your blessing.

(**SADIE** *zips up her suitcase.*)

SADIE. I can't, Asia. I just can't.

End Scene

Scene 3

(A museum. Sadie's quilts hang on the wall. [Note: The images of the quilts should be left to the imagination of the audience and should not hang on the walls.]

SADIE *stares up at them.* **NELLA** *and* **ASIA** *stand beside her.* **NELLA** *snaps a picture.)*

ASIA. Would you put that away? They gonna put us out of here.

SADIE. Says no pictures.

NELLA. They your quilts. You can't take a picture of your own quilts?

SADIE. Stop.

NELLA. Yours is the best.

SADIE. Hush. They all nice

NELLA. Still.

ASIA. They're beautiful, mama.

SADIE. They look so big up there on that wall. Don't they? On the bed they just look regular. But up there.

NELLA. These white folks is paying a lot of money to be looking at our trash.

ASIA. It's not trash anymore, Aunt Nella. It's art.

SADIE. It's like nothing I ever seen before. Look, there's my name.

NELLA. You famous now.

SADIE. We all up there, Asia. You, me and Mama. I take what my mother give to me and look where it is now. We had nothing else to give, but what we know. And we give it to you. You say Gee's Bend ain't give you nothing, you look up at them quilts. It's the cotton from that land holding those quilts together. Our blood and our tears melted into the seams. Them quilts could tell stories these people'll never know. They don't know the babies been born in them quilts, the people who died, the love that's been made. Little pieces of our lives sewn up in those quilts. Little pieces of our history. We made them, cause we had nothing else.

(**SADIE** *tries to hold back her tears.*)

ASIA. Mama, what you crying for?

SADIE. At the glory of it all.

End Scene

Scene 4

(Night. The front door is wide open. **SADIE** *is quilting. She takes her glasses off and wipes her eyes.* **ASIA** *enters.)*

ASIA. You still leaving the door wide open.

SADIE. It's nice out.

ASIA. We talked about this.

SADIE. And I said what I have to say.

ASIA. Mama, I'll get you a new lock.

SADIE. That one ain't broke.

ASIA. Then use it.

SADIE. I thought you was already gone.

ASIA. Had a few more things to pack. Wanted to come and say goodbye.

SADIE. Bye.

ASIA. I'm off on Thursday. I come pick you and Nella up for the doctor.

SADIE. No need in taking Nella to the doctor.

ASIA. She's got an appointment.

SADIE. I'm not carrying her all the way to town to have the doctor tell me something I already know. Nothing she got broke's something they can fix.

ASIA. She's getting worse, Mama.

SADIE. She happy in the world she's living in. Let her be.

ASIA. Then I won't see you til Sunday.

SADIE. Alright.

ASIA. When you gonna come see the new house?

SADIE. I get around to it.

ASIA. Don't be that way.

SADIE. I got things to do.

ASIA. You being stubborn.

SADIE. Maybe.

(Pause.)

ASIA. I know you bought my land.

SADIE. What if I did?

ASIA. Where'd you get that kind of money?

SADIE. It's my money, I do what I want with it.

ASIA. You might need it.

SADIE. What for? I got everything I need right here.

ASIA. You should have told me.

SADIE. It's my business.

ASIA. That's a lot of money.

SADIE. I got a mind to buy up the whole Bend. Then it won't matter none about that ferry. It come up on my shore, I tell it to go back where it came from.

ASIA. What you gonna do with all that land?

SADIE. Thought I might plant some winter squash.

ASIA. Now you know that's not what I meant.

SADIE. Same thing I been doing.

ASIA. I worry about you and Nella out here all by yourselves.

SADIE. We ain't all by ourselves. We got people everywhere. These are my people.

(**NELLA** *wanders in. She is frail. She smiles when she sees* **ASIA**.)

NELLA. Ain't mama pretty?

SADIE. She is.

ASIA. Nella, I'm going now.

NELLA. You coming back?

ASIA. Next Sunday. For church.

NELLA. I'm singing in church on Sunday.

ASIA. You are?

NELLA. People say I sing good.

ASIA. You do sing good.

(**NELLA** *sits in her chair and sneaks a piece of candy.*)

SADIE. You call me when you get home. Let me know you got there safe.

ASIA. I will.

(**ASIA** *and* **SADIE** *hug.* **ASIA** *leaves.* **SADIE** *watches her, the door still open.*)

NELLA. Cover me up.

(**SADIE** *covers* **NELLA** *with a quilt.*)

SADIE. You better now?

NELLA. Where this quilt come from?

SADIE. Done made it a long time ago.

NELLA. You need to get you a new one. This one old.

SADIE. Maybe.

NELLA. I make me a nice quilt. With lots of pretty colors.

SADIE. You know you can't sew.

NELLA. You teach me?

SADIE. I teach you.

NELLA. Promise?

SADIE. Someday.

NELLA. Tired, now.

SADIE. Getting late. Why don't you sing me your church song?

NELLA. You like my singing?

SADIE. I like your singing.

(**SADIE** *closes the door.*)

NELLA. (*singing*)
> *When all God's children*
> *Get together*
> *Oh what a time*
> *What a time*
> *What a time*
> *We gonna go down*
> *By the banks*
> *Of the river*
> *Oh what a time*
> *What a time*
> *What a time.*

(*Song transitions into* **SADIE**'s *final moment at the swamp.*)

End scene

Scene 5

(The Cyprus Swamp. **SADIE** *stands in her special place.)*

SADIE. Nobody be talking about no quilt is art. But I seen it
on the walls, so I know it be so. We used to talk about
all the places we'd go. Places I didn't never think I'd
see. But my quilts, they take me there.

*(She kneels down and digs in the dirt. From the earth
she removes an old mason jar. And inside that mason
jar is a key.)*

Sadie removes the key from the jar and examines it.)

WOMEN. *(singing)*
When the preacher
And the deacon
Get together
Oh what a time
What a time
What a time.

We gonna go down
By the banks
Of the river
Oh what a time
What a time
What a time

SADIE. I remember the dream that brought me to you,
Lord. I was so scared. But I had faith in you and you
protected me. You took me safely across that river.
You have brought me this far, Lord. You have reached
down and blessed me. I got things today I never dream
of. Things you have given. You have answered my
prayers.
I don't think that ferry ever coming.
But if it do, I be ready.

*(***SADIE*** *holds up the key)*

And I pray it be your will.

(**SADIE** *slips the key into her pocket.*)

WOMEN. *(singing)*
> *When the white folks*
> *And the colored folks*
> *Get together*
> *Oh what a time*
> *What a time*
> *What a time.*
>
> *We gonna go down*
> *By the banks*
> *Of the river*
> *Oh what a time*
> *What a time*
> *What a time.*

End play

Printed in the United States
220737BV00005B/1/P

9 780573 663673